How We Do a
48 Hour Film Project

TIPS FROM A MULTIPLE-YEAR ENTRANT
AND SOMETIME AWARD-WINNER

Michele Bousquet

How We Do a
48 Hour Film Project

Foreword

While studying in New York City in 1998, I read an article about two women who had started one of the first 24-hour theater competitions. I immediately thought, "That's cool!" and, "We should do that with video, but we're going to need more time. Something like 48 hours."

With that, the concept of the 48 Hour Film Project was born. It took three years for there to be widespread access to technology (inexpensive cameras and computer editing programs), and in May 2001, the first 48 was held in Washington, DC.

In this book, longtime 48er, Michele Bousquet, does a great job of walking you through the ins and outs of making a 48 Hour Film Project. "How We Do a 48 Hour Film Project" is comprehensive. It covers all of the rules and requirements and gives you insight into how Michele and her team created award-winning films.

As she points out, it is not always easy, and inevitably you've got to enlist your team's creativity when a surprise pops up. But most often the weekend is a lot of fun, and the 48 has helped launch many careers in the industry.

This book is a must read for those wanting to know more about the 48. Happy reading—and I hope to see your 48 Hour film soon.

Mark Ruppert
Creator and Executive Producer
48 Hour Film Project

Preface

I'll never forget my first 48 Hour Film Project, because it changed the trajectory of my life.

I'd worked in and out of the film industry in many ways over the years. In the 1980s, I worked as a Production Assistant on commercials, then became an editor for corporate videos. In the 1990s I worked as an animator at a TV studio, and in the early 2000s I was part of a two-person crew that went into rural areas and shot low-budget commercials. Then I moved into producing training videos for technical training. I wrote scripts, applied makeup, shot footage, edited videos, and even provided the odd animation to show how a product worked.

I also took some acting classes, and participated in independent theater and film productions. I particularly enjoyed improv classes, where I learned to come up with a quick quip for just about any situation.

Throughout all this, I never produced any narrative fiction of my own, nothing that was my imaginative creation from start to finish.

In the summer of 2019, I was living my best life with a steady job as a technical writer, the field I had finally settled into. Every few weeks I performed with my improv troupe, which included some of the funniest and most talented people I've ever met. We all became such good friends that we hung out together almost every weekend, even when we weren't performing. (If you want to have a Saturday night where you laugh so hard your ribs hurt, hang out with a bunch of improv performers.)

That summer, the 48 Hour Film Project popped up in my line of sight, and I had an idea. Instead of doing karaoke or seeing a play or whatever that weekend, how about we make a film? I'd shoot it on my iPhone and it would probably be terrible, but we'd have a great time, as we always did.

As for my expectations, I was in for a surprise. Two of my improv friends specialized in costuming and makeup on the side. Another had been gigging as a cinematographer, and showed up with all his gear including a light kit.

It was a crazy weekend, with barely any sleep and me and the cinematographer tag-teaming on shots and editing. Our Producer, an improv friend who had never produced anything resembling a film in her life, conspired with one of the actors to write a hilarious two-page scene to replace a dull two-liner, and it turned out to be the best scene in the film. I had picked my Producer for her organizational skills, but she really stepped up on that one.

The result was *Ride to Destiny*, a silly Western about people riding around on hobby horses looking for love. In the 48 Hour Film Project for New Orleans in 2019, *Ride to Destiny* went on to be nominated for 7 awards in a field of nearly 50 entries, and we won 5 of those awards, including Grand Prize Audience Choice.

You might say that *Ride to Destiny* created a monster, namely me. After that film, I got fired up about making more films, and even more. I entered contest after contest, sometimes doing great and sometimes bombing. No matter the outcome, each film was fuel to do yet another.

I started going to yard sales that offered costumes, and to this day I still pick up discarded electronics off the side of the road in case they came in handy as props for the post-apocalyptic blockbuster I will make one day.

In the year I write this book, 2024, I've just entered my 10th weekend competition. I am having so much fun making films, and I learn so much each time I make a new one.

Over time, my crew has shifted and changed, but we've all remained friends. Some have moved away, or have gone on to get so much industry work that they can't spare the time. Others keep coming back because it's just so much fun.

I hope that your journey into doing a 48 Hour Film Contest has all the joy that mine has had. It should be fun, and it should be a learning experience. Your first film might be terrible, but your next one will be better. And what better way to hone your skills than during a crazy 48-hour period?

It's a rush, it's exhausting, it's exhilarating, and it should be impossible, but it's not. I hope that through this book, I can help you get the most out of the 48 Hour Film Project, and that you'll enjoy it as much as I have throughout the years.

Michele Bousquet, Author

P.S. You can check out a full list of our films, and how they did in each competition, in the *Appendix*. Spoiler alert: They weren't all winners. But man, did we have a great time!

Contents

Introduction 1
What's it all about?. 1
Other weekend competitions. 3

Chapter 1: Preparation 5
Before you begin. 5
Review the rules 5
Find out which weekend it is 9
Register your team 9
Know how to contact your City Producer 11
Join the 48 Facebook page 12
Figure out your filmmaking process. 13
Get your equipment together 13
Figure out the video-to-editing process. 16
Consider optional items .18
Form your team 20
Find your team. 20
Line up your actors. 21
Pick a Kickoff Picker-Upper 22
Pick a Story Team 22
Figure out who does what 22
Essential roles 23
Additional crew roles. 24
Sample 12-person team .26
Sample four-person team. 28
Start a group chat 29
Get the rest together 30

Figure out locations 30

Figure out wardrobe. 33

Set your budget 34

Print out other agreements 34

FAQ 36

Chapter 2: Kickoff / Story 39

Brainstorm 39

Balancing ideas with available actors. 40

The Accordion Script 41

Solidify the story. 42

Take a lot of notes 42

Work in the requirements. 43

Finish up the story. 45

Write the script 45

Format the script. 46

Talk to your crew 48

Announce wardrobe/prop needs. 48

Spill the graphics needs 50

Get some sleep! 51

Chapter 3: Production 53

A typical schedule 53

Tips for a good production day 56

Chapter 4: Editing 59
Editing tasks. 60
 Editing task timing 62
Finalizing the Film 63

Chapter 5: Screenings & Awards. 67
Pre-screening screenings. 67
Official screening 68
 Getting the most from the screening 68
 Judge's Awards 71
After the Film 73
That's all, folks! 74

Appendix 75
Appendix A: Prep checklist 77
Appendix B: Films that won 79
Appendix C: All our entries. 83
Appendix D: Resources 95

Introduction

If you're reading this book, it probably means you've heard of the 48 Hour Film Project. Maybe you've signed up for one, or you're thinking about it. But just in case you've wandered here unawares, here's a brief introduction.

What's it all about?

The 48 Hour Film Project (or "The 48," as many of us call it) is a competition that takes place on different weekends in different cities throughout the year. Each team registers in a specific city, and makes a four-to-seven minute film in just 48 hours using a specific prop, character, and line of dialogue.

In the weeks leading up to kickoff, there are mixers where you can meet other filmmakers, and find cast and crew members for your team.

Then the contest weekend comes, with a kickoff at 7pm on Friday. Each team receives one or two unique genres, and all entries for that city receive the same required character, prop, and line of dialogue.

For the next 48 hours, it's a race to make the film with all the requirements, and turn it in by the required time on Sunday night.

It's an insane weekend where your filmmaking and leadership skills are put to the test.

If you do it right, you'll have a blast and learn a lot, and even make lifelong friends. And you just might make a decent film in the process.

A few weeks later there's a live screening of all the films, where you can marvel at what other teams have done and see how you stack up against them. Besides an opportunity to see some amazing films, you get to meet other filmmakers in your city and grow your network. This is also where the audience votes on their favorite films for the Audience Choice Award.

A few weeks after that, a panel of judges announces nominations for awards like Best Film, Best Actor/Actress, Best Use of Line, and a bunch of other categories.

Then there's an awards ceremony, a red-carpet event where the 1st, 2nd, and 3rd place awards are announced in each category. Trophies are handed over, speeches are given, and there's more networking.

It might seem like a crazy concept, but you'd be surprised at the amount of support, education, and joy this contest can bring. That is, if you go at it with the right attitude about what "success" is. That success might just be connecting with other filmmakers, learning something new, or making new friends.

Will you get rich and famous? Probably not. I have seen teams that went on to get film deals, and actors that went on to success in commercials and series, but the results are usually more modest. My editor, for example, got a lot more editing work after we did a 48, and the cinematographer who helped with my first 48 is now so busy that I have to book him months in advance if I want him for a shoot.

The 48 Hour Film Contest isn't about winning or getting recognized by Hollywood. It's about accomplishing something that seems impossible and improving as a filmmaker along the way. Winning is certainly nice, but if you make it about winning, you'll be miserable. Make it about learning or having fun, and you'll enjoy it a whole lot more, and will probably make a better film.

Other weekend competitions

The 48 Hour Film Project isn't the only limited-time film competition out there, and not the only one we enter.

The approach described in this book is the one we use for all our competitions, but the timeline is sometimes spread out over many more hours, days, or even weeks.

Most notable is The Kickoff 48*, an international 48-hour competition offered by the same organization that holds the 48 Hour Film Project. The competition takes place entirely online.

See the *Appendix* for more about these competitions, and for more about finding competitions you can enter.

---

* In 2025, The Kickoff 48 replaced the Four Points Film Project as the organization's international weekend competition.

Chapter 1: Preparation

Even though you can't start making a film for the 48 Hour Film Project until the kickoff on Friday night, you can do a lot of preparation before the big weekend, all within the limits of the official rules.

Before you begin

Even before you start to think about equipment and locations, there are a bunch of things you can do to kick off your entry into the 48*.

Review the rules

Before you start your preparation, be sure to review the rules of the 48. Be especially aware of what you can and can't do prior to kickoff, and the types of material that are allowed or disallowed in the film itself. The rules are posted well in advance of the 48 weekend, and are publicly available for review even before you sign up.

The rules exist to keep the spirit of the 48 Hour Film Project, which is to encourage people to actually make a film during that time. An extreme example of a film that violates the spirit

---

* Throughout this book, I'll refer to the 48 Hour Film Project as "The 48," which is how my crew and other teams refer to it.

would be one that consists of a series of photos taken prior to the 48 weekend, accompanied by a voiceover telling a story. The rules do allow photos taken prior to kickoff to be used to augment scenes filmed during the 48 weekend, but the rules also seek to prevent filmmakers from skipping the filmmaking part altogether.

The rules do get updated from time to time, so I'm not going to copy them here verbatim; you should review the rules as they stand when you're about to start.

There are a lot of rules, which can be overwhelming for a first-time team. To help focus your attention on the most important ones, here's a few notes on the types of rules I review newly each time I enter:

- *Film length.* The film has to be 4-7 minutes long. If your film is one second over the limit, it will not be accepted. There are specific rules about how credits may or may not be considered part of this time frame.

- *Pay (or lack thereof).* All participants must be volunteers. It's fine to pay for food, props, costume or equipment rentals, a round of post-production cocktails, screening tickets, and other expenses related to the film getting made and seen and everyone having a great time, but you cannot pay cast/crew directly for the job itself. This rule helps keep an even playing field between teams—it prevents wealthy or well-connected teams from hiring an Oscar-level DP who wouldn't otherwise participate, and limits teams to those who are in it for the experience and fun of it.

- *Permits to shoot in public.* The 48 Hour Film Project in New Orleans provides a blanket permit for shooting in public areas, but your city might be different. While this permit covers shooting on streets and sidewalks, it might not cover certain public parks. Be sure to check with your City Producer before choosing a public area as a location.

- *Previously shot footage and stock footage.* While all footage in your film is supposed to be shot over the 48-hour period (your "core footage"), there are exceptions for "supporting footage." See the rules for details.

- *Photos and stock images.* These are allowed under certain circumstances. In general, they need to support your "core footage" shot over the film weekend and cannot be used on their own.

- *AI-generated images and video.* There are specific rules around these now. In general, you have to have the rights to use such images, and they can't infringe on anyone else's copyright.

- *Music.* Royalty-free music is fine, provided you have a license or subscription or other clear evidence of permission. Previously recorded music is also allowed. Do not, under any circumstances, use copyrighted music that you don't have the rights for, as you will be disqualified from screenings and awards. Our favorite subscription site is Storyblocks.com, which has a ton of music and sound effects, but there's also a lot of royalty-free music available on YouTube.

- *Graphics.* While the rules at the time of this writing don't specifically mention graphics, they would presumably come under the umbrella of "images". Create your own graphics, or use royalty-free graphics that you have the rights to use. Sites like Pixabay.com are a great resource. You can also use graphics from a subscription site like Shutterstock or iStockPhoto, but only if you have a valid subscription.

- *Animation.* You can use scenes and characters you created prior to the 48-hour window, but all animation of such scenes and characters must be performed during the 48-hour window.

- *Required paperwork.* Every cast and crew member must sign a waiver, and you must have a release for every location you use, even if it's your own home. The paperwork is a beast the first time you do a 48, but it gets easier with subsequent submissions. In addition, the team leader must sign the Team Leader Agreement prior to kickoff. That's the only paperwork required to get started—the rest is due later in the weekend.

- *Required slates and credits.* Download the required slate video from the 48 website ahead of time and have it ready for your editing process. There's no rule that says you can't set this up before kickoff!

- *No prescreening distribution.* While it is hard (so very hard!) to not post your film to YouTube or another online service right after it's done, don't do it. Don't post it as Unlisted or Private on YouTube. Just don't. Instead, invite the cast and crew over to your house for a screening, or just suck it up. Do. Not. Violate. This. Rule.

It's silly to get disqualified over a violation that you could have easily prevented. Take the time during preproduction to get familiar with the rules, and refer to them during the weekend as needed. And don't go by my interpretations, as rules might change.

Remember that the 48 Hour Film Contest wants you to succeed. They want you to submit a film that can be screened and considered for awards. These rules are designed to make a fair contest for everyone, including you.

Find out which weekend it is

Your city's 48-hour weekend is usually announced several months ahead of time. Before signing up, make sure your Cousin Agnes isn't getting married that weekend, or that you aren't taking the Bar Exam or SATs or something. You might also check with a few potential crew members to see if they can make it that weekend.

Register your team

Before you can submit a film to the 48, you'll need to register your team. This means picking a team name and paying the fee. You will also have to designate yourself (or someone) as the Team Leader. This person is the primary contact for the contest, and the one responsible for turning in the final film. Usually this is the Director, Producer, or Screenwriter, but not always. Anyone can be the Team Leader as long as they're willing to take on the responsibility.

Registration typically opens a few months before the contest weekend, often alongside an announcement of the weekend dates.

Registration fees are usually in the $125-$200 range. The earlier you register your team, the cheaper the registration fee.

> **ABOUT THE FEES**
>
> Your registration fees, and the cost for tickets to the screenings, are not some kind of scheme for the 48 Hour Film Contest to get rich off you. When you consider how much time, effort, and resources go into producing the competition, and the returns you get in terms of learning, satisfaction, networking, and a chance to see some great films, it's a bargain.
>
> Registration fees go to the 48 corporate offices for infrastructure. All expenses to run and provide your city's 48 Hour Film Project come from ticket sales for local events.

Sign the Team Leader Agreement

Before the Kickoff on Friday night, you will need to sign a Team Leader Agreement. You must sign this agreement before you can get your team's genre and the city's prop, line, and character on the Kickoff night.

The Team Leader Agreement asks you to agree, among other things:

- ‣ That you will abide by rules about creating the film over the competition weekend.
- ‣ That they have the rights to show the film at screenings, on their website, etc.

- That you will secure any necessary copyright agreements for third-party sound and visuals appearing in the film.
- That when you screen the film at a festival or otherwise, you need to keep the 48 Hour Film Project logo or statement in your film.
- That they aren't responsible for any injury or drama resulting from your participation (standard damages waiver).
- That the 48 has rights to a percentage of any money you make off the film.

That last one might feel weird, but in reality, I have never made a dime off of any film I made for the 48. For whatever reason, Netflix has not been beating down my door to show my 48-hour film.

Please note that this is my interpretation of the Team Leader Agreement, and that you should read it for yourself to see what it says. And, of course, sign off only if you're willing to agree to the terms.

Know how to contact your City Producer

Your City Producer will be happy to answer any questions you have about the contest, whether before, during, or after the 48-hour weekend.

After you register, you will receive an email telling you how to contact your City Producer. If anything about the contact method is unclear, be sure to email back and ask.

Knowing how to contact your City Producer is particularly useful during the heat of the 48-hour weekend, when you think you might be in danger of violating a rule. Can you substitute a prop? Can you film in a particular park? Just ask. Your City Producer will respond quickly, and will be happy to help you make your film a success.

It's also a great idea to attend at least one of the pre-weekend mixers so you can meet your City Producer (and their assistant) face-to-face.

Join the 48 Facebook page

Your local 48 probably has a Facebook page. Find it, join it, and be part of the experience.

Our local 48 also has a second Facebook page just for filmmakers where you can post BTS pictures and see what other teams are doing.

Figure out your filmmaking process

The easy part is done. Now it's time to figure out what you're going to use to make the film, and how you're going to use it.

Get your equipment together

You'll need at least a little equipment to make your film. If you've already made a film or two, you know what you have and what to do with it. But if this is your first film ever, you'll want to make sure you'll have access to sufficient equipment for the 48 weekend.

Please note that this is not a comprehensive list of everything you'll ever need to make a film. This is just what we've found to be the bare minimum to make something decent.

- *Camera and lens.* It doesn't matter what camera or lens you use, as long as it shoots at least 1920x1080 (HD) resolution. You can use an iPhone, a high-end camera with a selection of lenses, or anything in between.

- *Media storage.* Cameras record to some kind of media, like an SD card or SSD drive. Whatever you record with, make sure you have the right media for your camera, sufficient storage space, and a way to move the footage to your editing computer. If you're planning to record on your phone, make sure you have lots of empty space on it for recordings.

- *Lights.* You can use any kind of lights for your shoot, even sunlight or lamps from around your house. Just make sure you have enough to light your scene.

- *Editing software.* If you don't already have a favorite editing package, you can explore some free options like DaVinci Resolve and iMovie.

- *Editing computer.* Set up a computer for editing ahead of time.

- *Sound equipment.* Don't rely on the camera's microphone—the sound will be very hard to clean*, which will greatly affect your film's quality.

  While sound technicians might argue for this equipment or that, you can get pretty decent sound from an inexpensive lavalier microphone (the kind you see clipped to the lapels of talk show guests, also called a *lav* for short). Several scenes in our film *Ride to Destiny* were filmed with a lav.

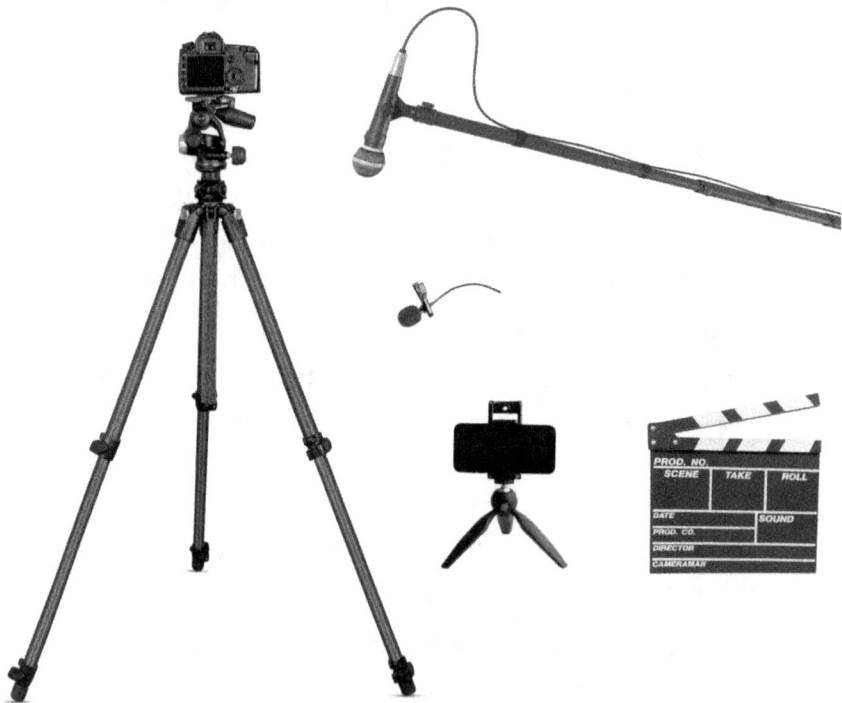

Figure 1: Equipment that comes in handy for a 48

* *Sound cleaning* is the process of removing the inevitable "hum" and other background noise from sound you've recorded. We'll talk more about sound cleaning in the next section.

Ideally, you have a directional microphone of some kind, but it's not strictly necessary to make a short film. Even the microphone on a cell phone, if held close to the actor's mouth when speaking, will give you decent sound.

You might also have access to a boom, a big stick with a directional microphone attached to it. If you do, great. If not, don't sweat it. You can get pretty good sound with what you already have.

The sound can be recorded on a separate media, or you can plug the microphone right into the camera for easier editing.

As with any equipment, test it ahead of time to make sure you know how to get the sound files onto your computer, and that your editor knows what to do with them.

And if you can't do any of these things, consider making a silent film, a music video, or a film that uses mostly voiceover. As long as you retain at least one of your required genres, these types of films are fine to submit.

▸ **Sound cleaning software.** No matter how you record your sound, you'll need to *clean* the sound. This means removing any hum or other distracting noise from the dialogue. Even the quietest room will have a low hum from lights and electronics.

You'll also need a way to *mix* the sound, meaning evening out the dialogue volume levels, and putting it together with music and sound effects. Usually, you can do this in your video editing software.

We consider sound mixing/cleaning to be a vital step in the filmmaking process. We use Audacity (free software) to clean out the hum, and to smooth out the volume's peaks and valleys.

Figure out the video-to-editing process

Well before the weekend arrives, make sure you know how you're going to get the video footage and sound into your editing software. The process can vary depending on the camera you use, your sound media, the type of PC you edit on, and the editing software you use.

If you're shooting with a camera that uses an SD card, for example, make sure you have an SD card reader handy for transferring footage to the computer. It's also a good idea to have at least three SD cards so you can copy one while shooting with another, and a spare in case one of the cards doesn't work. And make sure the SD card has sufficient speed to work with your camera. Not all SD cards are created equal!

If you're shooting on a mobile phone, make sure you have a surefire way to get the footage off the phone for editing. Test the footage and make sure you can use it with your editing software. You might find that you need to convert the footage to another file format before you can use it. There are free conversion tools available for this, but you should work that workflow out ahead of the 48 weekend.

Set up a folder structure on your PC for saving the files. Our folder structure looks something like this:

Film 48 Hour 2025

- ▸ *Video*
- ▸ *Audio*
- ▸ *Titles-Credits*
- ▸ *Renders*

Another consideration is the amount of time it takes to transfer files from camera to computer. There's nothing worse than having to wait two or three hours for files to transfer when you had planned on using that time for editing.

No matter which type of camera or audio equipment you use, it's wise to test the workflow before the 48 weekend and work out any kinks in the process, rather than wait until the weekend when you are rushed, stressed, and exhausted.

Consider optional items

Here are some additional items you might want to use during your shoot:

Tripod or other stabilization. While you can shoot your entire film in the handheld fashion, you might want to have a way to stabilize your camera.

Basic, functional tripods for phones and cameras are inexpensive and nice to have, but technically speaking, you don't need them. It's perfectly fine to rest the phone or camera on a table or a stack of boxes.

In the rush of shooting for the 48 weekend, we will often do just that, even though I own three tripods. Plopping the camera onto a table is quicker than fussing with a tripod, shortening the time to make a shot from 15 minutes to 5. Those extra minutes are precious during a 48!

Slate board. I shot my first two films without a slate board (clapperboard), and we did just fine. But then I got one, and Holy Moly! What a difference it made in the speed of editing. A clapperboard is especially important if your sound is recorded separately from your video (i.e. your microphone is not plugged directly into your camera).

Clapperboards are inexpensive, with the added bonus that first-timers will find it super fun to be the Official Slate Operator. If you order one online, be sure to check that it isn't intended to be decorative only, and that you can actually write on it with chalk or a whiteboard marker.

SHOULD I RENT EQUIPMENT FOR MY FILM?

If you don't have a camera, lights, tripod, or the right kind of SD card for your camera, you might be tempted to rent these things. If it's your first time doing a 48, I would recommend that you not rent anything and instead, use what you have available.

Put the camera on a stack of boxes instead of using a tripod. Bring household lamps for lighting, or shoot outside during the day when there's plenty of light for free.

And you can often borrow equipment, or ask the DP or Sound Tech to bring what they have handy.

Form your team

No matter what equipment you have, you need a team! A team can be as small as one person or can go as high as you want. A typical team size is 10-15 people. I've done it all by myself (one person) and gone as high as 20, but my preferred size is around 12 people total for cast and crew.

Find your team

How do you find your cast and crew? There are a lot of ways.

- *Tap your friends.* A few months ahead of the 48, tell your friends you're planning to do it and see who wants to participate. You might be surprised who steps up.

- *Go to a 48 Hour Film Project mixer.* Your local 48 holds these mixers prior to the 48 weekend. You'll meet others who want to join a team, and other Team Leaders who will be happy to talk to you about their experiences.

- *Join an acting class.* If you're an actor, tap a few other actor friends to join you. Promise each one they'll get a role if they fill a crew role as well. They might be terrible at lighting or camera work, but so what? And you never know, they might be great at it. Either way, you'll have a great time and learn something along the way.

- *Post a notice online.* If you have crew and just need actors, put up a post on social media, or visit a local improv class and ask who wants to play. Actors are the easiest to find! And improv actors are the best.

- *Do it alone.* If all else fails, resign yourself to doing it alone. You'll meet other teams at the screening, and find more people to get involved the next time around.

Be sure to get contact info for anyone who's joining your team. You'll need it for the group chat before you start.

Line up your actors

In order to effectively write the script, the screenwriter will need to know which actors will be available for the entire shooting day. If all you get is three grumpy old men, your script will revolve around those grumpy old men. If you have two people who could reasonably play a couple, that opens up an option for a family or dating drama.

Contact the actors and confirm with them a week or two ahead of time, and again a day or two before the 48 starts. People sometimes forget, or new commitments pop up. Some can only make it for part of the day, which limits their roles.

NOT EVERYONE WILL SHOW UP

On every 48 I've done, at least one committed person had to drop out at the last minute due to a family emergency or other urgent situation. While you can't plan for this, you can plan for having to adapt to it.

In 2024, we had three people drop out last-minute. But then the DP brought his girlfriend along, and she filled in for all of them like a pro. Plus, she shot some drone footage for the film! We had never had drone footage before.

The moral of the story is: *You never know what's going to happen during a 48*. This is part of what makes it so fun and exciting.

Of course there can be surprises, like an actor getting sick or having an unexpected emergency. Your screenwriter will need to keep the script adaptable just for such cases.

Pick a Kickoff Picker-Upper

As part of the Friday night Kickoff, someone from your team will need to physically go to the Kickoff event and pick up your genre and other requirements. Be sure to check the rules and announcements for details such as the time to show up, which is usually 6PM.

Pick a Story Team

Arrange for some team members to be part of the Story Team, the folks who will kick around ideas on Friday night until a story emerges.

Some teams do it with just 1-2 people, and some have 5-6 people or more. We usually invite 4-5 key people to this grand event. The first year we had 12 people, which was a bit much! We've settled on 4-5 as a good number that works for us.

Your first time, just invite whoever you want. The important thing is to have a good time exercising your imagination.

Figure out who does what

Around a week before the 48, I sit down with a handful of key people to figure out who will do what.

- ‣ The first step is to contact everyone who said they'd participate, and confirm that they'll still be coming.
- ‣ Next, write down a list of crew roles and assign a role to each person. This list can be just for yourself and not shared with anyone. Even if you're not sure Theresa can

do lighting or Mike can figure out wardrobe, go ahead and make your list as best you can. These roles might change on the 48 weekend, but at least you'll go into it with some semblance of a plan.

With a team of 10-15 people, the usual size, you won't have enough people for every role. However, it's a good idea to consider who will do each one.

Essential roles

These are the bare bones roles for producing a film for a 48.

- *Screenwriter.* Someone has to write the script on Friday night or Saturday morning.
- *Director.* The creative boss, directly involved in the shooting process, making sure the scenes look right, the actors are doing what they should be doing, and that the shooting gets done.
- *Director of Photography (DP).* Designs and records the shots on camera.
- *Actors.* The people who appear in the film.
- *Editor.* Puts the footage together into a finished film, usually on Sunday.
- *Document Wrangler.* Ensures all the required paperwork is completed and filed.

In a one-person team, that single person could do all these tasks in tandem, one after the other. With a team of 3-5 people, it wouldn't be unusual for the most experienced person to take on the Screenwriter, Director, DP, and Editor roles while everyone else fills in the gaps. It's all about what works best for you and your team to get the job done.

Additional crew roles

In a larger team, more roles can be assigned. These are the ones we assign with a 10-15 person team, in no particular order. Please note that these roles are in addition to the essential roles in the previous section.

- *Producer.* The logistics boss, directing traffic and making sure the creative folks (the Director in particular) can do their job without distractions. Controls the budget, deals with unexpected mishaps, and generally ensures that the film happens.

- *Craft Services.* In charge of food. Ensures meal, snacks, and drinks are available. Also known as *Crafty*.

- *Set Designer.* Determines how the set should look, and sources items to dress it appropriately.

- *Lighting Designer / Gaffer.* Sets up and controls the lighting during the shoot.

- *Sound Technician.* Records sound during the shoot.

- *Script Supervisor*. Follows along with the script during the shoot, assists actors with lines, and makes notes that can assist the editor after shooting is finished. Also known as *Scripty*.

- *Continuity.* Ensures that wardrobe, makeup, positioning of props, etc. are the same from one scene to the next.

- *Slate Operator.* The person who updates the clapperboard with the scene and take numbers, and clacks it at the start of each shot.

SLATE OPERATOR?

This isn't a real role in professional filmmaking—this job is usually performed by a member of the cinematography unit. But since your crew probably won't have enough people to assign this to just one person, clapperboard duties can be passed around between whoever doesn't have their hands full when a scene is about to be shot. Everybody likes to clack the clapperboard, especially new people. It's part of the filmmaking experience!

- *Wardrobe.* Chooses the actors' costumes and accessories, and helps them get dressed if needed.

- *Makeup / Hair.* Takes care of actors' makeup and hair.

- *Special Effects (SFX).* Applying special effects makeup, and working with the DP to line up shots for visual effects (smoke, fire, etc.) that will be added in editing.

- *Prop Master.* Finds or sources props, and ensures they're ready for shooting.

- *Composer.* Writes and produces music for the film.

- *Sound Designer.* Sources music and sound effects for the film, and helps the Editor incorporate them.

- *Sound Editor.* Cleans up the sound and aligns it with video footage.

- *Graphic Artist.* Creates graphic elements for the film, such as titles, logos, signage, and overlays.

- *Behind-the-scenes (BTS) photographer.* Takes photos and videos of the production process.

- *Production Assistant (PA).* A catch-all role for someone with no specific job, who pitches in where needed.

Sample 12-person team

If you've been counting, you realize that there are more than 12 roles listed in the previous sections. In our 12-person team, we stack the roles. Here's a typical breakdown:

	Main role	Also does...
1	Producer	Craft Services Document Wrangler Supporting Actor
2	Director	Screenwriter Co-Editor
3	Director of Photography (DP)	Lighting Design (Gaffer)
4	Sound Technician	Sound Designer Supporting Actor
5	Script Supervisor	Continuity Supporting Actor
6	Wardrobe	Makeup / Hair Special Effects (SFX)
7	Editor	Set Designer Sound Editor
8	Production Assistant 1	BTS Photographer Background Actor
9	Production Assistant 2	Prop Master Background Actor
10	Production Assistant 3	Slate Operator Background Actor
11	Lead Actor	
12	Lead Actor	

Figure 2: Chart of twelve-person team roles

Now we have a great 12-person team that can handle a one-day shoot with lots of flexibility.

I should note that having listed all these roles in a neat and tidy fashion, the reality is that everyone ends up doing everything. While the Sound Technician certainly stays on top of their job, in between you might find them up on a ladder helping the Gaffer, arranging set items or props with the Set Designer, in a corner running lines with an actor, or on set wearing a wig as a background actor (having handed off their sound duties to a PA for that shot).

It's not unusual for people to hand off some of their duties so everyone gets a chance to learn and play. For example, the Director can give over directing duties to the DP or even a PA for a scene or two, so they can see what it's like. It's all part of the experience of a 48.

In our shoots, pretty much everyone is also an Actor. Our 2-3 main actors often serve as PAs when they're not in a scene, and crew are often called in for minor roles.

CREW AS ACTORS?

In my team, just about everyone in the crew has at least a little acting experience. In fact, if an actor wants to join my team, my first question is, "Which crew role can you fill when you're not on camera?"

If someone doesn't want to act, I don't put them on camera. But more often than not, they're happy to pop in front of the camera for a line or two.

Sample four-person team

Short on team members? You can still do it! There will be a lot of doubling and tripling up, but many teams (self included) have done this. Here's how a four-person team could work:

	Main role	Also does...
1	Producer	Craft Services Document Wrangler Wardrobe Makeup / Hair Lead Actor
2	Director	Screenwriter Co-Editor Director of Photography Lighting Designer
3	Sound Technician	Sound Designer Continuity Slate Operator Supporting Actor
4	Editor	Set Designer Sound Editor Script Supervisor BTS Photographer Graphic Artist Lead Actor

Figure 3: Chart of four-person team roles

In reality, anyone on the team could be an Actor, or you could bring in people who just act. In my experience, finding people who just want to act is the easy part. It's finding crew that's tougher.

Start a group chat

Start a text thread with everyone who's committed to the team. While you can do this via text message, I prefer to use Facebook Messenger or WhatsApp as it's easier to add and remove people than with standard text messaging.

In the week leading up to the film weekend, talk about your plans and express your excitement about the upcoming weekend. Talk about plans like:

- *Locations you've secured.* Hey, this abandoned bowling alley gave us consent to shoot there! Or, here are the various rooms we can shoot in at the DP's house.

- *Who's the Kickoff Picker-Upper?* The 48 requires that someone from the team be physically present to pick up the genre. Assign this role before the weekend comes upon you, and make sure they know how to get there and when. This role is crucial to you starting the 48 as soon as possible.

- *Story team.* Who will come Friday night to brainstorm a story and script? After our initial year where we had 12 people spitballing on story and it was pretty wild, we try to keep this to 4-6 people so it doesn't get too crazy. How you choose to handle this is up to you. Be sure to coordinate with your screenwriter to ensure they have time to write the script after the story team is done.

- *Food preferences.* Discuss plans for Crafty, and find out if anyone has any dietary needs or food preferences so these can be ironed out ahead of time.

- ▸ *Shoot day info.* In the Group Chat you can post call times*, costume, makeup, and prop requests, and other important info closer to the shoot date, even the morning of the shoot. Make sure everyone knows to look at the Group Chat before they leave for the shoot.

Get the rest together

You're nearly there in your preparations! Just a few more things to figure out.

Figure out locations

In the real world of filmmaking, you write a story then find the locations to tell that story, but using that approach on a 48 just isn't practical. Scouting locations on Saturday morning just isn't feasible. By the time the locations sign off (if they do at all), half your weekend will be gone.

In a 48, it's best to do it backwards–you get access to some locations, and you write a script to fit those locations.

Whatever locations you choose, you will need a signed *Location Release* unless you are filming in a public place, like a street. Location Release forms can be downloaded from the 48 Hour Film Project website. The Location Release must be signed by the owner of the building, or someone who can sign on behalf of the owner. Sometimes the tenant or business owner can do this, such as a manager of a business, but in general, the working staff cannot.

---

* In filmmaking a *call time* is the time of day when you expect cast or crew to show up.

While you might love the idea of total freedom in your storytelling, where you'll magically find a retail store or an escape room or a castle on Saturday morning to shoot your fabulous story, the reality is that a Location Release can be challenging to get.

For one thing, the owner or manager of the property is very likely not going to be on the premises when you show up. To get permissions for locations, I have had to start two weeks ahead of time at minimum, and I often couldn't get a signature from a place that was just down the street from home base because the owner or manager is only there on random Tuesdays between 9:00 and 9:02 PM.

The 48 is stressful enough, why make it worse? The best locations are easily accessible and free to use. Consider these locations for your 48 film:

- Your own house or yard.
- A cast/crew member's house/yard.
- A friend or family member's house/yard.
- Outdoors on a public street or sidewalk. No Location Release needed!
- Your place of work.

A bar, restaurant, or retail store might seem like a great location, and they might even say, "Sure, come shoot here, no problem," but when you get there you find that:

- The door is locked and no one is coming for three hours.
- The A/C is ridiculously loud.
- They won't turn off the music.
- They limit you to two people inside at a time.
- They refuse to allow additional equipment beyond a camera (no lighting or sound equipment).
- The manager isn't there to sign the Location Release.
- You can only shoot for one hour.

All these things have happened to us.

If you're going to use a location like this, make sure they're on board for everything you need to do. And even then, you might want to line up a backup location in case something doesn't go as expected, such as bad weather for an outdoor location.

On the other hand, we've had great success with a couple of local places that are always happy for us to shoot there, and will bend over backwards to accommodate us. We've shot at one particular coffee house several times, and the owner loves us because we:

- Buy lots of rounds of coffee for cast and crew.
- Clean up any mess we make.
- Make his place seem a little more exciting to customers, with our cameras and clapperboards and calling out "Action!" every once in a while.

If you think you might want to use a restaurant, bar, coffee shop, etc. as a location, I strongly advise you to approach them at least two weeks ahead of time to get the owner/manager's signature. At the same time, take your measure of their enthusiasm. If they seem just-okay with it but don't seem to be willing to, say, turn off the music for a couple of hours, you should go elsewhere. If they get super excited and can't wait to have you there, that's a much better fit.

And they might give a verbal OK, but in the end they have to sign the release. When you turn in the film you need to turn in a signed Location Release for every location you used, or the film will be disqualified from screenings and awards.

Figure out wardrobe

Wardrobe is often overlooked in the preproduction process, but it might be worth checking out your options. This is particularly handy during the story session, when you need to create a story you can shoot with the resources you have at hand.

We are lucky to live in New Orleans, where people tend to have extensive costume closets. We also have a good friend who manages the wardrobe for several theaters in the area.

If all you have is modern clothes that the cast and crew will bring, that's fine. Just know this ahead of time so you can write your story accordingly.

Set your budget

Most of my 48s have cost about $300 to produce, with the following breakdown:

- ‣ *Food:* $250, which includes coffee, muffins, lunch, and dinner. Usually lunch/dinner is a sandwich platter from the grocery store plus chips, dip, and snacks.
- ‣ *Props:* $25. It's hard to estimate what you'll need, but you'll probably need something. On my films, props we had to buy included hobby horses (for a Western), eye drops (required prop), and specific makeup items for a special effect. The cost has never exceeded $25.
- ‣ *SD cards:* $25.

On my first 48, I asked everyone to put $10 in the pot to help cover costs. In later ones, I covered the cost myself. Do whatever works best for you.

With one film, we got lucky enough to have an investor who was happy to cover the costs in exchange for an Executive Producer credit. I've also heard of teams that got food donated by a restaurant in exchange for a "Thank You" credit. If you get lucky like this, be realistic about expectations for their return on their investment.

Print out other agreements

Ahead of the weekend, you can print out the waivers the cast and crew will need to sign, Location Release forms, and any other forms you might need. Put them in a nice folder or binder to keep them all together, and hand them to your Document Wrangler on the day.

Preparation roundup

While all this might seem like a lot, the good news is you don't have to do all of it. Do what you can, and let the rest ride. You're supposed to be having a good time, and if it becomes work, it defeats the purpose.

THINGS YOU CAN ASK PEOPLE TO BRING

My cast and crew often say they want to bring something to contribute to the process. Here are some things we have asked for:

Weird snacks. Sometimes people receive candy or snacks as a gift, but it's something they can't (or don't want to) eat. We ask our team members to bring in these snacks to share. This has made for some bizarre offerings, from mysterious Japanese candy to oddly shaped marshmallow treats and gum flavors I'd never heard of before. Why not make Crafty fun?

Toilet paper. I learned this one from experience. The 48 always seems to come around just when I'm down to my last roll. Asking a few people to bring a roll in with them isn't a huge imposition, and ensures that everyone is "comfortable" all day.

Bug spray. If you're shooting outside in the summer, the bugs can ruin everyone's good time. Having a few extra cans of bug spray around can make all the difference.

I've included a checklist in the Appendix to help you tick off the items as you prepare. If you don't get to all of them, it's fine.

Relax, you've got this! It's just a film.

FAQ

Here are a few common questions I often hear about the 48 and other time-limited competitions.

How do I make a film that's sure to win?

Hahaha. If I knew the answer to that question, my team would win every time.

There's no way to guarantee you'll win Best Film, or any award for that matter, no matter what you do. Judges have their own minds, and I've watched them pass over what I thought was a brilliant film in favor of one I didn't like at all.

I've also been the other end of the stick, where our team won an award that surprised me.

Judges be judges, and that's just the reality of any art competition. Do your best work, produce a film your team can be proud of, and accept the judges' decisions graciously. Congratulate the winners, and make friends with them as part of your networking.

I've heard about bad experiences people had with the 48. How do I know my team won't go through that?

I've heard these stories too. These "bad experiences" had to do with getting yelled at for no real reason, or waiting around for hours while the Director and DP screamed at each other for no real reason. This is no fun, but it's common enough that several of my team members were reluctant to join our team because of such experiences in the past.

My take on this problem is that you get it when (a) key crew (including the Team Leader) are overtired and (b) they have a "We must win!" attitude. That's when you have irritable, demanding people getting crabby with their volunteer cast and crew. It's not a good look.

I know some teams stay up all weekend, but we don't. This is one way we avoid getting cranky and demanding. You're supposed to be enjoying the experience, and being so tired and irritable that you start barking at people does not make for a fun environment.

If you're the Team Leader, you can set boundaries to ensure everyone has a good experience. Let the cast and crew know ahead of time that this is not meant to be a blockbuster film, that learning something and enjoying the experience are just as important as producing a good film.

As another safeguard against a bad experience, I have a "safe word" for my Producer to say to me if I become a bit too demanding or unpleasant with the team. (I'm proud to say that she's only had to use it once. I chilled out and apologized, and all was well.)

What's to stop teams from cheating?

I hear this question from newbies sometimes. By this they mean a team writing the script ahead of time, or shooting footage beforehand.

My question back is, "Why would anyone want to?" While I've heard of teams cheating a handful of times, I don't understand it. The 48 exists to challenge you and your team to grow as filmmakers, and to make your team proud of accomplishing something in just 48 hours, something that seemed impossible just a few days before. Cheating is the opposite of this.

I suppose a team might cheat to try and get awards, but that just sounds ridiculous. The only monetary award for the 48 is $500 for Best Film (not exactly life-changing money) and the rest of the awards are trophies or certificates. They're going to cheat to get a trophy? What are we here, six years old?

So don't worry about cheaters. They're few and far between, and their guilt probably makes them grumpy and miserable at the screening instead of cheerfully meeting other filmmakers and making connections.

Chapter 2
Kickoff / Story

Ah, Friday evening. It's 7:03PM, and your designated Kickoff Picker Upper has just texted you the requirements:

- ▸ **Genre.** Two choices, different for every team.
- ▸ **Line of dialogue.** A short sentence which must be spoken verbatim. Same for every team in your city.
- ▸ **Prop.** An everyday object. Same for every team in your city.
- ▸ **Character.** The character requirement includes a name and occupation. Same for every team in your city.

Now it's time to brainstorm with your Story Team.

Brainstorm

The story brainstorming session starts the second the Story Team gets the requirements on Friday night

For us, the session typically goes for 2-3 hours. During that time, we work to come up with a story that has a beginning, a middle, and an end. We also need to consider:

- ▸ **Locations.** The story has to be doable in the locations for which we already have a signed Location Release, or are 100% sure we can get one over the weekend.

- *Sets and props.* Do we have the props to turn our living room into a disco? Can we make the front of Carl's house look like a butcher shop?

- *Lead actors.* Our lead actors are always among the ones that can come for the entire shooting day (Saturday) and stay into the evening if needed, and even pop in on Sunday just in case. We write for the actors we have—if all we have is an 80-year-old man in a wheelchair and a pregnant 20-year-old, then they're the stars of the film. We try to have a selection of five to six lead actors of different ages and genders so we have a little more freedom in our story development, but often we have only two or three.

- *Supporting actors.* Before you write a big dance scene or a party scene, consider whether you have enough actors to fill the scene. On the flip side, if you have a lot of actors who just want a little something, consider writing in a group scene where everyone gets a moment in the spotlight.

- *Wardrobe.* Most 48-hour films set the scene in present day, so modern clothing is fine. When figuring out your story, the main thing to consider is whether you can scrounge up the space suit or clown costume that your story calls for. We live in New Orleans, the home of Mardi Gras, and thus have accumulated an extensive costume collection, but not everyone has.

Balancing ideas with available actors

Balancing the script with the number of actors available (and who are expecting a part when they show up) is a tricky business.

For our 2021 entry *The Critic*, we thought we had enough actors to play the customers at the center of our story. At the last minute we realized we needed just one more person, so we got the Sound Designer's girlfriend, who was just there to hang out, to put on a costume and do a five-second bit on camera. It went great and we got our shot.

On the flip side, I know of a team that ambitiously wrote a story that involved a large, raucous party without having more than a handful of actors lined up. They spent a large part of Saturday calling up every actor they knew, taking away valuable time that they could have spent shooting the film.

The Accordion Script

Some teams set the number of actors ahead of time, and that's that. Personally I like to write what I call an *Accordion Script*, where the script has room to grow or shrink depending on the number of actors who show up.

In *Butterfly*, our 2024 submission, the "accordion" consisted of several short social media clips where wannabe influencers got to have their say. That same year, the entry *Two Jakes and a Mug* had a party scene where lots of people got a line. On the other hand, one of the best films that same year, *Special Delivery,* featured just two actors. It just goes to show that teams can roll differently, and that's all fine.

For us, it's always a balancing act between the story we want to tell and the actors we have available, and even actors who are coming to help as crew with the expectation of a line or two.

Making all these variables work is part of the 48-hour challenge.

Solidify the story

It's hard to describe the story session. I wish I had recorded some of ours!

Ideas fly around. Someone suggests a story about witches who do macrame, another about an accountant who dresses like Santa. An idea about a big-box retail store is shot down because we don't have time or props to build a set, and another about a shipwreck because we don't have a boat. In fact, ideas are brought up and shot down every two minutes, either due to logistics or lack of vibe with the team.

But a few ideas stick, the ones that make everyone sit up with excitement. Out of these sticky ideas, a story starts to form. We start to picture certain actors playing one part or another. We're pretty sure Natasha has a mime costume, or that Jamil has a collection of bison and deer figurines we can use for that pivotal moment when Ingrid realizes she loves him after all. And if we shoot that scene at sunset, we can aim the camera down the street over there and get a great silhouette shot…

It's impossible to describe how the story forms. I'm not even sure how it happens myself. All I can tell you is that it happens. Along the way we more or less cast an actor to play each important role, also keeping in mind that we might need to swap in someone else if the actor doesn't show up.

Take a lot of notes

Make sure someone is noting down all this brilliance, as the screenwriter will need these notes when they sit down to bang out the script.

Work in the requirements

During the story session, the required line, prop, or character will often be the spark of an idea. But after that, you need to work in the rest of the requirements.

You can get creative with these requirements. And sometimes, "creative" is better.

Incorporating the required character

The character is often the most challenging one to incorporate into your film. The character must be physically present in at least one scene, and must be identified through references to the character's occupation, first name, and/or last name.

Figuring out a non-awkward way to do this can be hard! The way a lot of teams deal with this is to make the required character the main character, which makes referencing the character's occupation and name more natural.

Other teams take a more creative approach and have the required character as a side character. More than once I've seen the character revealed to be a dead body in the corner, verbally referenced by name and occupation.

It's worth noting that you don't always have to reference both first *and* last name to meet the character requirement. For example, suppose the required character is Bob or Bobbie Smith, a plumber. So you have a guy wearing overalls and a name tag that reads "Bob," and he walks in holding a wrench and asks, "You got trouble with your pipes?"

Because the judges know they're looking for Bob Smith, a plumber, the judges can definitely tell that that's the guy, even without his last name being mentioned.

You can also interpret the character's occupation loosely. In the 2024 New Orleans 48 Hour film *Special Delivery*, where the required character was a postal worker, they made one of the main characters a process server who had quit being a postal worker the day before. We also saw the film *Postal Apolcalypse* where a survivor of a viral scourge delivered packages she found while scavenging, effectively turning her into a postal worker.

Note that graceful references to name and occupation will score higher with judges than clunky, on-the-nose references. For example, with Bob the Plumber, the scene I described earlier would score higher than a dude saying, "Hello, I am Bob Smith, and I am a plumber."

If in doubt, you can always ask your City Producer to confirm that what you have in mind meets the requirement.

Incorporating the required line

The required line is definitely a place where you can get creative. In the New Orleans 48 Hour Film Project in 2019, the required line of dialogue was "We're going paperless." We were making the Western *Ride to Destiny*, with our two lead actors galloping around town on hobby horses. How could we possibly work in that line without forcing an awkward conversation about paper conservation?

One of our story team had the brilliant idea to name the lead character's horse "Paperless" so the character could shout, "Come on! We're going, Paperless!" when she exited a scene. It got a good laugh from the audience, and more importantly, it met the requirement without clashing with the rest of the film.

Some films meet the line requirement seamlessly, and some have an awkward moment where the line was clearly shoved in. Either way, get it in, however you do it! It's part of the whole experience of the 48.

Incorporating the required prop

The prop is usually an everyday object like a chair or a water bottle. But sometimes it can be challenging if you pull Western or another genre that calls for a period piece, during a time when the prop didn't exist.

One notable example is in the 2021 New Orleans 48, where the required prop was a laptop. That year, the team *I'm Your Density* pulled Western as a genre. They wanted to make a period film that took place in a saloon, and they didn't want to have a laptop computer suddenly show up in the scene.

The team came up with a creative solution: they interpreted "laptop" as the top of a person's lap, with one character saying to another, "Come sit on my laptop." During the 48 weekend, they checked with the City Producer that this usage would fit the requirement, and went on to win Best Use of Prop in the awards.

Finish up the story

Back to the story session on Friday night. After 2-3 hours of idea-shouting, hand-waving, and jumping up to act out an epic scene, you just might have a solid story. In my experience, it's kind of like microwave popcorn: the ideas pop frantically for a while, then peter out as the story reaches completion. Somehow, everyone instinctively knows when we've got it.

Write the script

Now that you have a story, it's time to write the script. At this point the story team goes home and the screenwriter (or writers, plural) sits down to pound the keyboard.

Someone has to actually type it up into a script. Some teams write the script as a group, while other teams have a single writer. Some write it in a few hours, others stay up all night.

HOW LONG SHOULD THE SCRIPT BE?

The rule of thumb for a script is "one page per minute of finished film." This means your script should be 4-7 pages long to meet the 48 requirement of a 4-7 minute film.

There are numerous screenwriting courses so I won't get into the mechanics here, but all of them mention a beginning, middle, and end, and a conflict with a resolution.

From what other teams have told me, the script can take them anywhere from 3 to 12 hours to write. I write for 3-4 hours, from whenever the story team leaves (usually around 9PM) to 1AM or so, then go to bed and wake up at 8-9AM with some new additions in my head, and I type away for 1-2 hours more. I need the sleep so I can direct the next day, but I also know teams with a dedicated scriptwriter who writes all night. Whatever works for you and your team.

Format the script

Ideally, the screenwriter formats the script in a standard (or near-standard) way, but in my early days of 48s I sometimes skimped on the formatting and just got something out that we could use. It's such a short script that this has worked out fine, rather than me wasting precious time trying to make the printed script look like it came out of Hollywood.

At the very least, it's a good idea to number the scenes so you can reference them more easily during shooting and editing. I use Final Draft to write the script and easily number the scenes, but you can do this manually in Microsoft Word or Google Docs.

There are a lot of references online about how to format a screenplay, so I won't list them out here. But as an example, here's a short excerpt from our 2024 entry *Butterfly*, complete with scene numbers that helped us organize our shooting and editing processes.

```
14          INT. DANCE STUDIO - MONTAGE - FLASHBACK              14

            The studio is draped with black.

                            ANDREW
                    Thank you for coming to the
                    audition.

            Sarah dances.

                            ANDREW (CONT'D)
                    You'll do just fine.

            Andrew puts a cloth over Sarah's mouth. Sarah gasps.

15          EXT. ANDREW'S HOUSE - DAY                            15

            Jake knocks on the door. He is holding a package and the
            signing gizmo.

            Andrew opens the door.

            Jake hands him the package and the gizmo.

                            JAKE
                    Please sign here, sir.

            The tapping noise starts.

            Jake registers the sound.
```

Talk to your crew

Now that you know what you're going to do starting Saturday morning, it's time to hop on the Group Chat and talk to your crew before you crash for the night.

Announce wardrobe/prop needs

After writing the script, I send out a text to the Group Chat outlining what we'd like actors and crew to bring for their call time on Saturday. This would include these items, as they pertain to the story and shoot:

- Costume options.
- Props.
- Set dressing elements.
- Makeup.

In addition to telling people what to bring for wardrobe and makeup items, this is a great way to get the props you have in mind. ***Can someone bring a stuffed animal, preferably a duck? Who has a policeman's hat? Does anyone have a small Buddha statue?***

I generally ask cast to bring their own makeup so we don't have to worry about sanitary issues.

Tell the cast and crew to review the asks on Saturday morning before coming in for the shoot, and to load up their cars with anything that might help. This way, if you're still snoozing when your cast and crew wake up, they can review the list and respond with what they can bring, then load it up in their car while you're still making your first cup of coffee.

For example, when we made **The Critic**, we knew we would need a lot of Mason jar-type containers. Several people on our team brought some, and that gave us enough to fill up the store windows for the two sellers of Nut and Butter Spreads. The "nut and butter" in the jars was actually just water and food coloring.

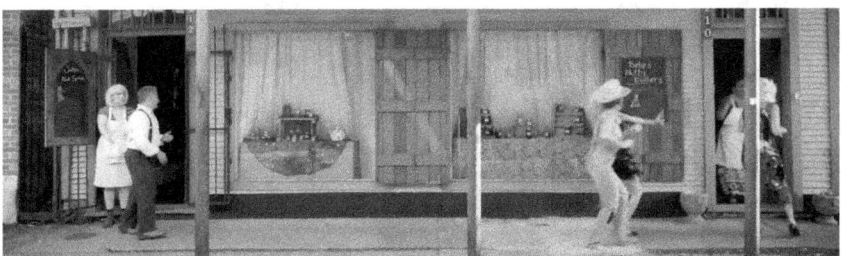

*Figure 4: Storefront in **The Critic***

When we made **Butterfly**, the required character was a postal worker. One of the cast happened to have a postal worker shirt, and he packed it up in his car and brought it along. Other teams did just fine with a blue shirt and a name tag.

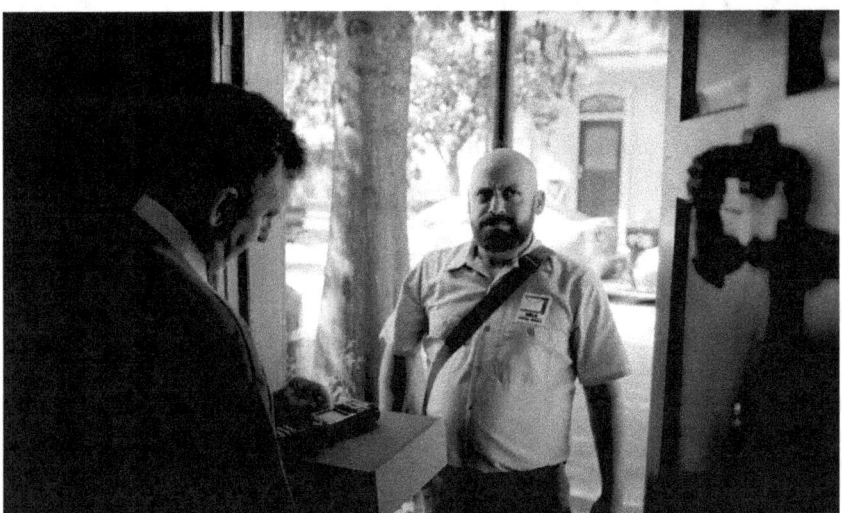

*Figure 5: Scene with postal worker from **Butterfly***

Spill the graphics needs

On Friday night, after completing the script, I send a separate text to the Graphic Artist regarding graphics and titles we'll likely need. This gives them a heads-up so they can start assembling the graphics.

For **Butterfly**, we needed social media-style overlays, and our artist, Dan Isaacs of Impish 8, got busy creating them.

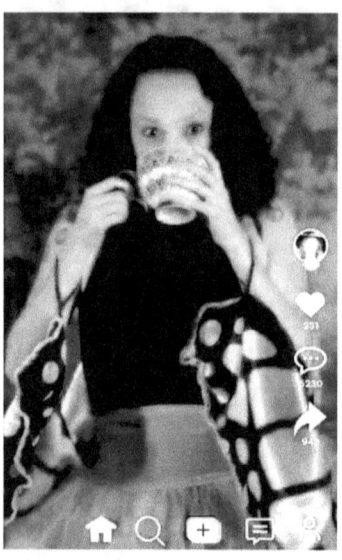

*Figure 7: Social media overlay from **Butterfly***

On **The Critic**, I asked Dan to create silent-film type titles for the final edit, and he delivered in style.

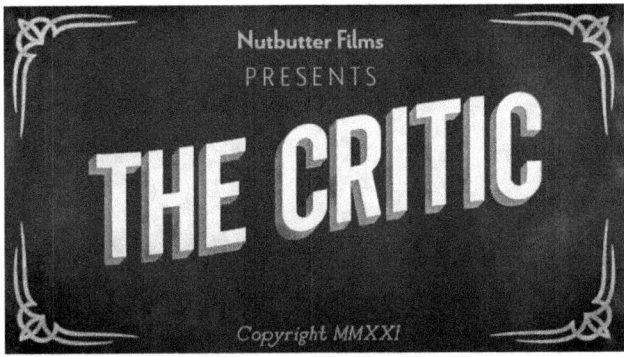

*Figure 6: Credits from **The Critic***

Get some sleep!

While some teams stay up for the entire 48 hours, we don't roll that way. Even 4-6 hours of shuteye does me wonders, and keeps me pleasant and sane as I work with the lovely volunteers who are giving their time to make a film with me.

If you want to stay up for the entire time, that's your decision. But please don't compromise your health and sanity. After all, it's just a film.

IT'S JUST A FILM

Say it louder for the people at the back: It's just a film!

You're not curing cancer, or saving babies from burning buildings. It's just a film.

The film might be great, or it might be a clunker. If it's not exactly Oscar material, the outcome will not affect your reputation or career in any meaningful way. Trust me on this one. It's just a film!

Chapter 3
Production

It's Saturday! The big shooting day. Quite possibly the most stressful day of your life. Relax, you'll survive.

A typical schedule

Every team is different. Some shoot all night Friday, others shoot all day Saturday and into Sunday. I provide our typical shooting schedule as a potential guideline, but certainly do whatever works best for your team.

Saturday 8-10AM

- Scriptwriter wakes up with six new ideas, puts them in the script, and prints out scripts for all cast and crew.
- Director puts together a rough shooting schedule.

THE SHOOTING SCHEDULE

In a real (paid) production, the shooting schedule is neatly laid out as a color-coded spreadsheet or grid, with the location, time to shoot, actors required, and so on.

In a 48, there usually isn't time to make up a nice color-coded schedule. Instead, there's a scribbled scene list, and we usually do the scenes in chronological order unless there's a good reason to do otherwise.

10AM

- ▸ Cast and crew arrive with their costumes, makeup, and props, and see the Wardrobe and Props people to figure things out for the day.
- ▸ Craft services sets up coffee and snacks.
- ▸ Scripts are distributed.

10AM-12PM

- ▸ Wardrobe and Makeup get the actors ready for shooting. When not in Wardrobe or Makeup, actors review the script, read over their lines, rehearse with one another.
- ▸ DP and other crew meet with the Director to go over the script and shooting schedule.
- ▸ Gaffer starts lighting the first shot.
- ▸ Director communicates to Graphic Artist regarding graphic elements.
- ▸ Document Wrangler gets everyone to sign a release.

12PM

- ▸ Craft services organizes lunch.

12PM-1PM

- ▸ We start shooting scenes.

1-1:30PM

- ▸ Break for lunch. Sometimes this is a "rolling break" where half the cast/crew take lunch while the rest of us keep working, then we trade off.

2PM-6PM

- ▸ More shooting.
- ▸ Record any voiceover.
- ▸ BTS photographer gets some photos.
- ▸ We take a 15-minute break every 1.5 hours or so, so we don't wear ourselves out.

6PM

- ▸ At this point we're winding down. Some take a break for dinner (provided by Crafty), while others are free to leave.

7:30PM

- ▸ Last shot of the day. This is the "Martini shot" where we allow cast and crew to enjoy a cocktail during the shot.

8PM

- ▸ It's a wrap! Everyone takes 30-60 minutes to toast the end of the shoot, socialize, help clean up the set.

8:30PM

- ▸ The Editor sneaks off to start editing.

9PM

- ▸ Cast and crew say goodbye, and leave the Editors to do their work.

Tips for a good production day

Here are some informal rules I abide by to have a good production day.

Feed your people

When I invite people to participate in a 48, I tell them that lunch is part of the deal. It's the least I can do! If they stay past 6PM I also feed them dinner, and offer beverages during the last shot.

Assemble a cast/crew list

Have a PA go around and get the correct spellings of everyone's names, and how they want to be credited. Most crew will work more than one job, so find out which one they want the major credit for. Bonus points if the PA types it all up in a Word document for easy conversion to credits during editing.

Create a pleasant working environment

Your cast and crew have volunteered their time to help you make your film, so you should respect them and their time. Praise them often for a job well done, and treat them well.

A 48 is supposed to be fun. Your volunteers do not deserve temper tantrums or other uncomfortable situations. Maybe you're tired and frustrated, but so what? They might stick around to finish, but they won't work with you again.

Listen to their ideas. Sometimes the ideas will be ridiculous, but sometimes they'll be amazing.

Take a deep breath, be nice, listen. It costs you nothing.

Double-check requirements

It's easy to get caught up in the shooting process and forget some important things, like the requirements.

When I directed *The Critic* and we got to the end of a long and exhausting shooting day, I was about to let everyone go home. My Producer, Charity Cosme, requested that we review the script one last time to make sure we had everything we needed.

We discovered, to my horror, that we had forgotten to shoot the required line of dialogue. The required line! I quickly called the two main actors onto the set to shoot a scene with the line, and all was well.

I am forever grateful to my Producer for making that call. The moral of the story: Get good people around you, and listen to them!

Chapter 4
Editing

Editing is just as important as shooting. A good edit can make the difference between a golf clap and thunderous applause.

Editing is accomplished with software like Adobe Premiere, DaVinci Resolve, Final Cut, or iMovie. We used to use Premiere, but switched to Resolve a couple of years ago because it's easier to use and has more features.

Some teams start editing when the shoot ends, while other teams have a dedicated Editor who starts as soon as the first shot rolls off the camera, and works all night to have something ready for Sunday morning.

Some have one Editor, some have two or three. As for us, we have two editors. One is also the Set Designer, and he starts editing late Saturday afternoon as soon as he's done with the set. Then the second Editor, me, is also the Director, who is busy until the last shot is finished. We take turns with the edit, with one sleeping while the other cranks away on the film.

However you do it, you'll need to get the film edited.

What if I don't have an editor?

The Editor role is perhaps the hardest for any team to fill. If you can't find an Editor, why not do it yourself?

Basic editing isn't that hard. There's free software and plenty of YouTube videos to help you. You're basically taking your shots and assembling them into a sequence to make a film.

Becoming an expert Editor takes years, but learning enough to make a decent short film takes just a few days.

Our Set Designer learned editing by going out and shooting footage of local bands, and making videos for them. That, and lots and lots of YouTube videos. And now he is our primary Editor for our 48s.

Editing tasks

At its core, editing is throwing clips on the timeline and putting them in sequence. But if you want your editing process to go smoothly, there are other tasks you'll need to do.

Here are the tasks we perform as part of the editing process, roughly in the order we do them:

> ▸ *File naming.* Renaming all the video and sound files to reflect the Scene-Shot-Take they correspond to. This is an extremely important step that saves a huge amount of time in editing. We usually name our files like *09.02.03.mp4* for Scene 9, Shot 2, Take 3.

- *Sound cleaning.* Cleaning up the sound files to remove the inevitable hum from the A/C, electronics in the room, and the general sounds of life.

- *Sound synchronization.* Lining up the sound files with the video files (if you didn't record with the camera microphone).

- *Music.* Gathering up appropriate music, whether from a royalty-free music site, YouTube, or a Composer.

- *Sound effects.* Bells, whistles, burps, thuds, ringtones, chirping birds, and any other sounds you need. If we can't find them from our royalty-free subscription site or free on YouTube, we do a quick recording.

- *Special effects.* If we need a fire effect or a splash of water or blood, we need to find it on our royalty-free subscription site, or create a quick substitute.

- *Last-minute shots.* Occasionally we'll run out (or ask someone to run out) and shoot some supporting footage. Usually it's a building, a street, or some other easy shot.

- *Last-minute voiceover.* We like voiceovers for the 48 for a little bit of extra context with low effort, a lot of bang for your buck. While most actors don't stick around for the editing process, an actor can record a quick voiceover from home on their phone, and email it to us. My editor and myself have also become adept at faking other people's voices for a line or two.

- *Graphic elements.* We have a dedicated graphics person on almost every shoot. He loves making the titles, overlays, and other graphic elements that bring the film to the next level.

COLOR GRADING

Color grading is the process of altering the colors in your raw footage to make it really pop. Every major motion picture performs extensive color grading, and you can find many "before and after" examples from these films with a quick Google search. It's actually quite amazing to see how color grading can move a scene from "Meh" to "OMG!"

Many 48 teams don't color grade their films, so you can set yourself apart by reserving an hour or two of the editing process for color grading. Popular editing software packages like Adobe Premiere and DaVinci Resolve include free color grading tools. While we never have time to make it perfect, we try to do at least a quick-and-dirty color grading to make it look better.

Editing task timing

Some editing tasks can be started on Saturday. Ideally, an Editor can start transferring files, naming them, and backing them up as soon as a few shots are complete.

We start this process as early as we can. These tasks that aren't that difficult to do, and starting them early can gain you lots of precious hours for the editing process.

If you can pull a computer-savvy person from the crew to do these tasks while shooting is still going on, all the better. That same person can also start cleaning sound, or putting shots on the timeline.

It's also helpful to have someone start scouring your royalty-free sound library for appropriate music and sound effects.

ROYALTY-FREE MUSIC ON YOUTUBE

One of the first surprises I encountered on a 48 Hour Film Project was the discovery of royalty-free music on YouTube. There are many content creators who post their music on YouTube, for free, with the offer to use their music for just the price of a mention in the credits.

I didn't know these creators existed until one of my Editors for *Ride to Destiny* pointed it out. That same year, we won the "Best Sound Design" award, all with music and sound effects legally sourced from YouTube.

Finalizing the Film

The home stretch in the few hours before the film is due can make or break your entry. Here is the timeline we operate from on the Sunday when the film is due:

Sunday 8AM-12PM

- Footage is placed in the timeline with major timings in place.
- Sound is cleaned.
- Music and sound effects are selected and put on the timeline.
- The Document Wrangler checks to make sure they have all the required documents, and chases up the ones that are missing. This isn't part of editing, but it's still important.

12PM-4PM

- Work on the timing of scene starts and ends, music, and sound effects.
- Plop in the credits, and the required start and end titles.
- Around 4PM, we have a decent edit, something we could turn in if we absolutely had to.

4PM-6PM

- Render and review, and make a few final tweaks.
- Render, review, render, review. In between renders, grab a snack. Remember to eat!

IF IT ISN'T IN DECENT SHAPE BY 4PM...

Our rule of thumb is that if we don't have a decent edit by 4PM, something that we could turn in if we absolutely had to, we won't make the 7PM deadline for upload. This has been true for every 48-hour film we've ever made.

6PM

- Upload the final film for submission well in time for the deadline.
- If you have time, make last-minute adjustments and upload a second or third version by the deadline.

8PM-MIDNIGHT

- ‣ Upload all the documents.
- ‣ Make a toast to completing the film. You did it! Pat yourself on the back.
- ‣ And get some sleep.

Chapter 5 Screenings & Awards

After the film is submitted, take a breather. In just a few weeks, your film will be screened!

Pre-screening screenings

Before the official 48 Hour Film Project screening, you can't share your film publicly. However, you can show it privately to the cast and crew, or to a group of friends. Consider holding a "screening night" at your home a couple of days after the end of the contest.

My rule of thumb is that I can show it to someone *in person* using hardware in my personal possession, such as my phone or laptop, but I can't share it on social media.

On social media you can share BTS photos and videos, or a 45-second trailer for the film.

Don't violate the rules by posting the film on YouTube or Vimeo, even as a Private or Unlisted video. Cast and crew might beg and plead that "I just want to show it to my Mom!" In that case, they can come over to your house and do a Facetime or Zoom while you play it on your phone or laptop.

Don't jeopardize the entire team's chances at awards by giving in to one team member. Stick to the rules.

Official screening

The official screening is perhaps the most exciting part of the 48 Hour Film Project. Your cast and crew, especially first-timers to the film business, will be very excited to see the film on the big screen. It doesn't matter if the film is terrible. They will be excited anyway. And really, who cares if it's great, mediocre, or terrible? You made a film (You Made a Film!!!) and that's a huge feat in itself.

The official screening takes place 2-3 weeks after the 48 weekend ends. Your City Producer will organize a screening at a proper theater with a big screen. This event includes time for mixing and socializing before and after the screening, for photographs, and for voting for Audience Choice awards.

The screenings are broken up into groups, with 12-15 films in each screening group. The groups are labeled Group A, Group B, etc.

The Team Leader gets two free tickets to their group's screening, but any additional tickets for cast/crew need to be purchased at around $15-$20 each.

Getting the most from the screening

The screening is a unique experience. It starts with a mixer in the lobby area, and a designated wall where you can take team photos. The mixer is where filmmakers swap war stories and generally meet and greet.

There's an amazing energy at these screenings that's hard to describe. Inside the theater, teams tend to sit together in small (or large) clutches. You'll see groups getting into a sort of high from seeing their work on the big screen, which is a beautiful thing all on its own.

CONSIDER TREATING YOUR TEAM TO TICKETS

I like to have a full crowd pulling for us at the screening, so every year I offer to pay for my cast and crew's tickets to the screening. One or two people take me up on it, while the rest purchase their own tickets. The idea is that some of my loyal cast and crew truly can't afford that extra $15-$20 for the ticket, and I don't want them to miss out. Of course there's a risk that some of them will read this book, in which case I just want to say, I am happy to pay for your ticket so you can come and be part of the experience.

Some of the films will be wonderful in some way, and some will be downright awful. Some will have some single surprisingly interesting element, while others will have an intriguing, original story. Some will use the prop in a way that makes you jealous that you didn't think of it yourself. Yet another will have an actor that you find very appealing for reasons you can't explain. There is something to learn from every film, every single one.

The most common problem you will notice is poor sound. Recording and cleaning sound is a big deal, and not everyone has the skill or capacity to deal with it. It's a sad fact that a lot of otherwise intriguing or appealing 48-hour films are beleaguered with poor sound.

Regardless, you should applaud for *all* the films. These people made a film, and turned it in on time. That, in itself, is a huge achievement. Clap, and clap loud. They made a film!

After each screening is finished, the films' Team Leaders will be invited up to the front of the room to talk about their films. This is an opportunity for the audience to get to know them, and to ask questions.

After the screening is more time for another mixer, which is a great time to comment to other filmmakers on their work, and exchange contact info. These are your peers, your fellow filmmakers, so meet and greet with abandon. Compliment actors on their performances. Ask the director how they managed to get that shot, or where the props came from. Friend each other on Facebook, and take selfies. Have fun!

Audience Choice Awards

At a group's screening, you'll be given a slip of paper with a list of that group's films. At the end of the screening, you will use that slip of paper to vote on your choices for the Audience Choice Award.

This award is completely separate from the judge's choices for all the other awards, as the winner is chosen entirely by the audience. However, the winner gets a trophy at the awards, just like all the judge's awards do.

I'd be lying if I said I didn't always vote for my own film for Audience Choice. But my two other votes go to the ones that I feel truly deserve it, and those votes are given a lot of weight as well.

> **AUDIENCE CHOICE AWARDS ARE ALWAYS UP FOR GRABS!**
>
> You might think that the Audience Choice would be a cut-and-dried decision, but think again. Even if a team brings a large group, each person still has to vote for three choices. For the 2024 selections, for example, my Editor and I marked different favorites for our two other votes. You never know with Audience Choice!

There is a second screening and voting session for the Audience Awards Championship at a local theater. The top three teams from each group compete separately, and the favorites are announced at the Awards Ceremony.

Judge's Awards

The Judge's Awards are separate from Audience Choice, and more numerous. But first, the nominations.

Nominations

The next big event after the screening is the public announcement of nominations for various judge's awards, usually a couple of weeks after the screening.

The Judge's Awards have various categories, which can include:

- Best Film
- Best Actor
- Best Actress
- Best Story
- Best Editing

- ▸ Best Sound Design
- ▸ Best Costumes
- ▸ Best Use of Prop
- ▸ Best Use of Line
- ▸ Best Use of Character

...and sometimes more categories, depending on what the judges deem fit.

The nominations are usually announced in a public forum such as the 48-hour city's web page or Facebook page.

Any particular 48-hour contest might include all these awards, and also many others. The contest folks reserve the right to add or subtract awards as warranted. For example, if several films use original music, they might want to nominate two or three teams for "Best Original Music". But if only one team uses original music, they might skip that award.

Awards Ceremony

The next big event after the nominations is the awards ceremony a few weeks after the nominations are announced. This event can include an actual red carpet to walk down, and dressing up is encouraged. The energy at this event is just as high as at the screenings.

Along with the announcement of the winners and awarding trophies, this event includes the screening of a few nominated films. And there's usually some photo opportunities, or even a dedicated photographer for the event.

This event is a great networking opportunity, especially if your team is screened and wins an award or two.

After the Film

After the film is finished, you have a lot of choices for what to do with the film.

- *Post it publicly.* Once the screening is over, you can post the film publicly on YouTube or Vimeo so your cast and crew can share it with friends and family. You might also opt to include it in your reel or portfolio.

IS IT OKAY TO DO MORE EDITS BEFORE POSTING THE FILM?

I often do a light edit on the film before posting it publicly. This gives me an opportunity to clean up a few things that got missed, things like a fade that went wrong or a credit that was left out. While I wouldn't advise making huge edits to the film before posting it (such as adding an entirely new scene), in my opinion it's okay to clean it up a little before posting it. I've never heard otherwise, so will continue to do so.

- *Show it at a festival or screening.* In New Orleans, there's a monthly Movie Mingle that shows locally made short films in an informal setting. It's a fun place to meet other filmmakers and see their work, and our actors often bring friends and family to see their performance. We've shown a number of our shorts at the Movie Mingle, including a couple from 48 contests.
- *Put it up on IMDB.* Putting your film on the Internet Movie Database website (IMDB.com) is a great way to give credit to your cast and crew, credits they can use to get future work.

- *Create a "Making of" film.* If you have enough BTS footage and pictures, consider making a short film detailing your experience. Apparently new filmmakers love to watch these films—our BTS "Making of" film for contest entry *A Common Thread* has three times more views on YouTube than the film itself!

- *Do it again.* While The 48 might be over for the year in your city, you can always travel to a nearby city for their 48 weekend and do it all again. The 48 organization also holds The Kickoff 48, where you can compete against international teams. You can also check out other time-limited competitions in your area.

That's all, folks!

Even as I write these words, we are planning to enter more contests. I'll keep updating the book as we continue on with our obsession with filmmaking. I wish you the same amount of joy, laughter, learning, and networking that we've gotten out of our experiences.

Appendix

Here you'll find information mentioned throughout the book.

Appendix A: 48 Prep checklist

Use the checklist to prepare before the big 48 weekend.

Appendix B: Films that won

Some of our films won awards. Here's a list of them.

Appendix C: All our entries

A list of all the short films we've made for contests, with context around each one. Some were gems, some were clunkers, but we keep making them anyway.

Appendix D: Links and resources

This section lists online links to all the contests and media that we mention in the book.

Appendix A
Prep checklist

Here's a handy-dandy checklist you can use to prep for your 48 weekend.

- ‣ Review the rules
- ‣ Register
- ‣ Sign Team Leader Agreement
- ‣ Join the 48 Facebook page
- ‣ Form a team
- ‣ Figure out equipment
- ‣ Test editing process
- ‣ List team members and roles
- ‣ Pick a Kickoff Picker-Upper
- ‣ Pick a Story Team
- ‣ Start a group chat
- ‣ Determine locations
- ‣ Print out releases
- ‣ Organize Crafty
- ‣ Send out call times, wardrobe/makeup, prop needs on group chat

After that, it's write a story, shoot, edit, submit!

Appendix B
Films that won

Here's a list of our films that were nominated or won an award.

If you want more context on our process, or want to see a list of all the films we made for competitions (not all of which won awards), see Appendix C. If you'd like to see these films, they're available on our YouTube channel:

Many Worlds Productions YouTube channel: youtube.com/@manyworldsvideo

I'd like to remind you that it's not about the awards. Still, it's nice to win something now and again, or at least be nominated.

48 Hour Film Project New Orleans, 2019
Entry: *Ride To Destiny*
July 26-28, 2019

- ‣ Audience Choice Grand Prize
- ‣ Audience Choice 1st Place, Group B
- ‣ Best Writing
- ‣ Best Costumes
- ‣ Best Sound Design

Nominations

- ‣ Best Actress: Jolene Magee
- ‣ Best Musical Score
- ‣ Best Use of Line

New Orleans 47 Hour Film Free-for-All 2020
Entry: *Magician Killers*
March 6-8, 2020

- ‣ Best Film, 3rd Place

48 Hour Film Project New Orleans, 2020
Entry: *Gadgets*
October 16-18, 2020

- ‣ Best Use of Line

48 Hour Film Project New Orleans, 2021
Entry: *The Critic*
August 13-15, 2021

- ▸ Best Film, 3rd Place

Nominations

- ▸ Best Editing
- ▸ Best Ensemble
- ▸ Best Sound Design
- ▸ Best Choreography
- ▸ Best Costumes
- ▸ Audience Choice Award

Four Points Film Project, 2022
Entry: *A Common Thread*
Nov 11-14, 2022

Nomination

- ▸ Audience Choice Finalist

48 Hour Film Project New Orleans, 2024
Entry: *Butterfly*

June 7-9, 2024

- ‣ Audience Choice Group A, 2nd Place
- ‣ Best Special Effects

Nominations

- ‣ Best Supporting Actress
- ‣ Best Makeup
- ‣ Best Graphics
- ‣ Best Set Design
- ‣ Best Choreography

7in7 Film Competition
Entry: *Shifting Tides*

June 17-24, 2024

- ‣ Best Use of Location

Appendix C
All our entries

I won't pretend that every film was a winner, but I will say that we learned something valuable on every single one.

Here's a chronological list of every film Many Worlds Productions has entered in competitions, and the context around each film.

Many of these films are available on our YouTube channel:

Many Worlds Productions YouTube channel:
youtube.com/@manyworldsvideo

48 Hour Film Project New Orleans, 2019
Entry: *Ride to Destiny*

July 26-28, 2019

Awards

- ‣ Audience Choice Grand Prize
- ‣ Audience Choice, Group B
- ‣ Best Writing
- ‣ Best Costumes
- ‣ Best Sound Design

Nominations

- ‣ Best Actress: Jolene Magee
- ‣ Best Musical Score
- ‣ Best Use of Line

This is the film that started me on my journey as a narrative filmmaker.

I was part of an improv troupe at the time, and we were all pretty tight, getting together almost every weekend to bar-hop or do karaoke or whatever. I suggested that instead of all that, we should instead spend this one weekend making a film.

Someone showed up with a camera, someone else showed up with cowboy gear, and we made a silly Western about a cowgirl looking for her destiny on the wild streets of New Orleans.

To my shock and surprise, we won a lot of awards and got a lot of praise for our efforts. And thus it began: My obsession with making short films for contests.

New Orleans 49 Hour Film Free-for-All 2019
Entry: *Reverence*
November 1-3, 2019

- ▸ Screened at Screamfest Nola 2024

The Free-for-All was a contest that local New Orleans production company Comfy Stone ran over the time-change weekend with the same parameters as a 48: genre, character, prop, and line.

From my *Ride to Destiny* team hardly anyone was available for that weekend, so I did most of it myself, playing two out of the three characters in a very sad film about a young woman trying to survive in a post-apocalyptic world. I didn't finish the film to my satisfaction by the deadline, but there were other good things that came out of it.

This contest only gave 1st, 2nd, and 3rd Best Film prizes, and I didn't win any of them. However, the audience feedback was great, and one of the judges strongly encouraged me to finish the film.

Because of that, and because I fell in love with the premise, I developed *Reverence* further, adding scenes and casting some wonderful young actresses to replace me. The final version of the film was screened at ScreamFest New Orleans in October 2024.

New Orleans 47 Hour Film Free-for-All 2020
Entry: *Magician Killers*

March 6-8, 2020

Awards

- ‣ Third Place, Best Film

Literally one week before the COVID-19 pandemic hit, local New Orleans production company Comfy Stone ran this contest over the spring time-change weekend with the same parameters as a 48: genre, character, prop, and line. This contest only gave 1st, 2nd, and 3rd Best Film awards.

We got the genre True Crime, and made a mock TV episode, loosely based on the *Homicide Hunter* series, about a rooming house where magicians tend to disappear. Because everyone involved was from my improv troupe, it ended up being a comedy.

The screening happened the day after the contest ended, but the prize ceremony was put off due to the sudden lockdown. Eventually the ceremony was held online in July 2020.

The film was a blast to make, and I still love to quote the iconic line "Esme is from Fraaaance!" at every opportunity.

Global Film Challenge 48-Hour Film Contest 2020
Entry: *Safe Hex*
June 12-14, 2020

During a brief respite from pandemic concerns of 2020, when we naively thought the worst was over, we entered this contest with a complicated script about witches and witch hunters.

Although I love the performances in this film, the set was beleagured with insurmountable sound issues and personal drama between team members.

We also had problems with multiple locations, including a store that wouldn't turn off the music and asked us to leave after an hour. At an outdoor location, one of our PAs was attacked by fire ants. Then there was the last-minute replacement actor, hopelessly drunk, who insisted on speaking in overblown Shakespearean tones because "It's acting!"

It wasn't our finest work, and understandably it didn't place in the rankings. Thankfully, we can laugh about it now.

48 Hour Film Project New Orleans, 2020
Entry: *Gadgets*

October 16-18, 2020

Awards

- ‣ Best Use of Line

With the pandemic postponing the usual August date but still a concern in October, I decided our team should skip the competition for the sake of everyone's health and sanity.

Then I woke up on Sunday morning with an idea, so I did my own "four-hour film contest" in my home. That's right, four hours! I made a four-minute film completely on my own, and had a great time doing it.

I expected nothing from this film other than the satisfaction of having made it. Winning an award was just a bonus.

48 Hour Film Project New Orleans, 2021
Entry: *The Critic*
August 13-15, 2021

Awards

- ‣ Best Film, 3rd Place

Nominations

- ‣ Best Editing
- ‣ Best Ensemble
- ‣ Best Sound Design
- ‣ Best Choreography
- ‣ Best Costumes
- ‣ Audience Choice Award

On the heels of the pandemic, my cast and crew were itching to get busy. But amidst concerns about closed spaces and microphone contamination, we decided to make a silent film (no microphones!) and do it outdoors (lots of air!), while still satisfying the given genre "Food Film."

The plot centered around two merchants in the 1930s competing for business. Turning it into a black-and-white period piece gave us the freedom to use costumes of all colors without concerns about clashing.

The Critic was super fun, and got us our first Best Film nomination.

48 Hour Film Project New Orleans, 2022
Entry: *Hare Today, Gone Tomorrow*

Aug 12-14, 2022

While this film turned out pretty well overall, we had some issues that caused us to turn it in late, which meant we were ineligible for awards.

We invited a new DP who used a different camera with huge files that we didn't test with the editing process ahead of time, which caused editing and rendering to take forever. We also had a cast member, a new addition to the team, who caused massive amounts of drama.

Lessons were learned, and we moved on. Still, not a terrible film. Just late and full of drama, which is not how we like to roll.

If you've been reading along through all this, you've gotten the message that personal drama amongst the cast and crew is a film killer. On this film, we learned that we need to choose our cast and crew carefully. While we love giving opportunities to new people, it can't be at the cost of ruining everyone else's experience.

Four Points Film Project, 2022
Entry: *A Common Thread*
Nov 11-14, 2022

Nomination

- ▸ Audience Choice Finalist

The Four Points Film Project was an international three-day (77-hour) film competition that used to be offered by the 48hfp folks in November of each year. After doing a 48-hour film, 77 hours felt like a leisurely pace!

This competition was our first foray into virtual production, with projected backgrounds reminiscent of Medieval England. We limited our cast and crew to people we knew well. It was a blast for everyone involved, and we learned a ton about filming with virtual production.

We also made a BTS (behind-the-scenes) video about the film, which somehow has three times the YouTube views of the film itself. Apparently a lot of people are learning about virtual production these days! I'm very glad to have contributed to this community with our BTS video.

The Four Points Film Project no longer exists as a 77-hour contest; it was replaced by The Kickoff 48 in early 2025.

Louisiana Film Prize 2023
Entry: *The Last Influencer Standing*

June 2-4, 2023

- ▸ Screened at Screamfest Nola 2023

For this one, we moved to a different track. When we realized we wouldn't be able to enter the local 48 due to family commitments, we entered a much larger state contest with a big prize: $25,000 for First Place.

Louisiana Film Prize gives you nine months to make a film up to 15 minutes long. We spent months on pre-production and post-production, and eventually produced a campy horror film using virtual backgrounds. The entire film was shot over a single weekend.

We're very proud of the result. For one thing, the plot revolves around scammy influencers who get murdered for their transgressions. Who can argue with that?

The film also gave us the opportunity to expand our network as we hired cast and crew outside our friend group. Some of those new people have become enthusiastic members of our core filmmaking group, and even our close friends.

We didn't make the finals for the contest, but the film was selected for the Screamfest Nola festival in October 2023, which gave us many networking opportunities.

48 Hour Film Project New Orleans, 2024
Entry: *Butterfly*

June 7-9, 2024

Awards

- ‣ Best Special Effects
- ‣ Audience Choice Group A, 2nd Place

Nominations

- ‣ Best Supporting Actress
- ‣ Best Makeup
- ‣ Best Graphics
- ‣ Best Set Design
- ‣ Best Choreography

This time, we attempted something outside our usual comedy genre: a serious film about human trafficking. At the same time, we're a bunch of improv actors who can't help injecting humor into this very grave topic.

The competition was intense. There were a lot of excellent films, and I was surprised we did as well as we did.

My favorite part of the experience was at the screening, when we spotted teenagers from the award-winning entry *The Grind* in the hallway recording each other doing the social media "Butterfly Challenge" from our film. Pure gold.

After we posted the film on YouTube, a local producer contacted us for a collaboration on a feature film, so there's that too.

7in7 Film Competition
Entry: *Shifting Tides*

June 17-24, 2024

Award

- ‣ Best Use of Location

This competition to make a 7-minute film in 7 days is an offshoot of our local Abita Springs International Film Festival. We tried something new, with a four-person crew (all of them cast as well) shooting a film on a boat. I wrote the script, then sent the crew off to shoot it.

The film came out pretty well, with some awesome drone shots that clinched the prize we got.

Appendix D
Resources

This Appendix includes links mentioned in the book.

Contest links

48 Hour Film Project: 48hourfilm.com/

The Kickoff 48: 48hourfilm.com/kickoff48

Royalty-free content

Pixabay.com - Free royalty-free images. Lots of good stuff.

Storyblocks.com - Our subscription site of choice, with images, videos, sound effect, and music. We can usually find what we need there.

Our published films on YouTube

Many Worlds Productions YouTube channel: youtube.com/@manyworldsvideo

Our public channel includes the following films:

- ‣ *Ride to Destiny* (2019)
- ‣ *Magician Killers* (2020)
- ‣ *The Critic* (2021)
- ‣ *A Common Thread* (2022)
- ‣ *A Common Thread BTS* (2022)
- ‣ *Butterfly* (2024)

On our channel, you'll also find our other work like behind-the-scenes and making-of videos, and several videos about our processes with virtual production.

Unpublished films on YouTube

These are films we don't make public. I include them here so you can see that they're not all gems, and some are just learning experiences. All are set to Unpublished on YouTube, but I'll let you watch them if you want. Watch at your own risk!

- ▸ *Safe Hex*
  youtu.be/jhwTNw27w3Y
- ▸ *Hare Today, Gone Tomorrow*
  youtu.be/2OqMdlpmUpw
- ▸ *Shifting Tides*
  youtu.be/qRfUPm7Ls9Q

Films you can't see yet

These films are still making the rounds of festivals, so we can't make them public just yet. One day, we'll unleash them on the world.

- ▸ *Reverence* (2019)
- ▸ *The Last Influencer Standing* (2023)

www.ingramcontent.com/pod-product-compliance
Lightning Source LLC
Chambersburg PA
CBHW052328220526
45472CB00001B/323